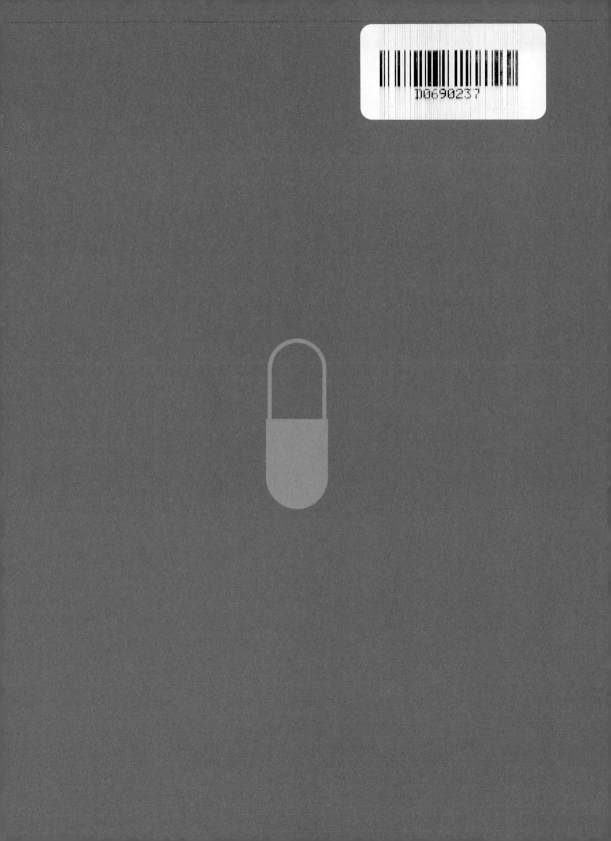

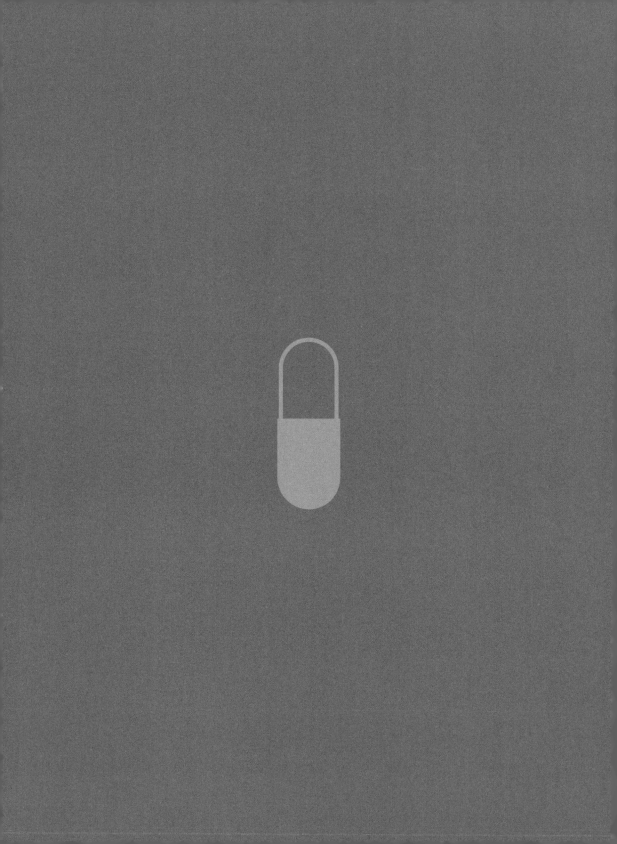

THE SELF-HELP SMORGASBORD

AN ACTIVITY BOOK FOR PEOPLE
WHO NEED ALL THE HELP THEY CAN GET

KNOCK
KNOCK.®
knockknockstuff.com

Created and published by Knock Knock
Distributed by Who's There Inc.
Venice, CA 90291
knockknockstuff.com

© 2012 Who's There Inc.
All rights reserved
Knock Knock is a trademark of Who's There Inc.
Made in China

ISBN: 978-160106364-9
UPC: 825703-50059-2

20 19 18 17 16 15 14 13 12 11 10 9 8 7 6 5 4 3 2 1

THE SMORGASBORD

Get enough sleep ....#1

Try meditation ....#2

Visit an acupuncturist ....#3

Take care of your oral hygiene ....#4

Talk about your feelings ....#5

Do some "fun" exercise ....#6

Avoid meat ....#7

Commit random acts of kindness ....#8

Create a scream box ....#9

Get a pet ....#10

Learn a martial art ....#11

Tap into your inner child ....#12

Face a fear ....#13

Do yoga ....#14

Behold the power of positive thinking! ..#15

Wake up early ....#16

Drink (really) fresh juice ....#17

Take up gardening ....#18

Drink tea ....#19

Volunteer ....#20

Believe in something ....#21

Get a massage ....#22

Self-medicate ....#23

Go to therapy ....#24

Ride a bike ....#25

Take a vow of silence ....#26

Make your bed ....#27

Breathe ....#28

Visit a psychic ....#29

Do some chanting ....#30

Unplug..#31

Create a relaxation ritual ....#32

Consult a guru ....#33

Move those legs ....#34

Go organic ....#35

Ask for help ....#36

Have sex ....#37

Simplify and declutter ....#38

Make a bucket list ....#39

Deprive your senses ....#40

Go forth and travel ....#41

Remember to smile ....#42

Restrict your diet ....#43

Get a makeover ....#44

Write in a journal ....#45

Indulge in a little schadenfreude ....#46

Take up a hobby ....#47

Go to a 12-step meeting ....#48

Practice feng shui ....#49

Treat yourself to a favorite food ....#50

Go outdoors ....#51

Practice acceptance ....#52

We all want to be our best selves:
smart, thin, funny, rich, and, perhaps most importantly, happy.

Unfortunately, there's probably something wrong with you. Hell, there's probably a lot wrong with you—and it's most likely holding you back. Whatever the magnitude of your shortcomings (from garden-variety quirks to certifiable personality defects) there's always something that interrupts achieving the holy grail of self-improvement: contentment.

If it's any comfort, at least you're not alone. (Or, as comedian Lily Tomlin once speculated, "We're all in this together—by ourselves.") The robust growth of the self-help industry is proof of our collective self-dissatisfaction: a grand total of 4,000–5,000 new self-help books are published annually, and the entire sector generates almost $1 billion per year.

Unfortunately, it seems as if having so many self-help resources at our disposal today is actually hindering our forward march toward satisfaction. The staggering array of available options is bound to make you feel overwhelmed and defeated—even worse off than before you began your quest. How can you possibly be expected to do all the things the psychologists, spiritualists, personal trainers, and former sports stars recommend? Is it even possible to drink that much tea (and wheat grass) while avoiding toxic people (and actual toxins) on a sixty-minute jog (outdoors) as you mentally repeat affirmations (that you're pretty sure you don't buy in the first place)? In a word, no. If you're attempting to satisfy every so-called essential of personal growth, you'll be far too tired and frustrated to feel anything remotely close to contentment.

Until now.

With the help of this journal you *can* do it all—by dipping one toe in at a time. The pages herein cover the basics of becoming a better you in baby steps, and contain everything you need to give each notion, potion, and common-sense strategy a shot over the span of a year—one weekly technique at a time. Best of all, this journal encourages you without any of the patronizing and often contradictory advice so frequently found in self-help guides and workbooks.

From basics like using your legs and talking about your feelings to advanced strategies such as acupuncture and sensory deprivation, the weekly prompts accompany full worksheets that describe what to do, how to do it, and how not to screw it up. Just take it one self-improvement at a time. By diligently sticking to something once a week, you'll increase your odds of finding something that actually works. You can jump around the book, picking and choosing what sounds most appealing, or follow the flow and go by page order. Either way, by the end of the year you may just achieve what you've been seeking all along: happiness. As the Rolling Stones famously sang, "You can't always get what you want. But if you try sometimes, you just might find, you get what you need."

GET ENOUGH SLEEP

☐ GO TO BED EARLIER ☐ WAKE UP LATER ☐ NAP

WHAT IS ENOUGH SLEEP?

Experts recommend getting seven to nine hours a night to maintain proper physical and mental function.

WHY DO IT?

Getting the requisite amount of sleep boosts cognitive function, mood, and disease immunity.

WHAT TO DO

1. Calculate necessary retiring and rising times

2. Lay supine

3. Close your eyes

4. Go to sleep

WAYS TO PREVENT FAILURE

Create a soothing sleep environment

Avoid caffeine in the afternoon

Invest in a quality mattress

Count sheep

SLEEP GOALS

1. Feeling rested

2. Improved mental faculties

3. Reduced under-eye bags

4. Escape

5. Other

FOR THE WEEK OF: ⬭

LEVEL OF:

RESISTANCE
- ☐ Kicking/screaming
- ☐ Mildly hesitant
- ☐ Mildly intrigued
- ☐ Curious
- ☐ Already an old pro

DIFFICULTY
- ☐ Sheer torture
- ☐ Herculean
- ☐ Formidable
- ☐ Manageable
- ☐ Child's play

ENJOYMENT
- ☐ Ecstatic
- ☐ Revelatory
- ☐ Harmless
- ☐ Irritating
- ☐ Cheerless

BENEFITS	DRAWBACKS
1.	1.
2.	2.
3.	3.

OVERALL IMPRESSION

☐ INSTANT NIRVANA ☐ SOME (SELF-) IMPROVEMENT ☐ MEH

FIX-YOURSELF FACT

According to the Mayo Clinic, more than a third of adults have sleep-related issues at one point or another, and 10 to 15 percent currently suffer chronic insomnia.

TRY MEDITATION

☐ MINDFULNESS ☐ ZEN ☐ WALKING

WHAT IS MEDITATION?

An ancient and spiritually founded internal process meant to promote positive qualities such as contemplation, tranquility, and self-awareness.

WHY DO IT?

Meditation has been proven to help in management of stress and physical pain; anecdotally, it can also provide a serene aura that is enviable to less "enlightened" individuals.

WHAT TO DO

1. Determine the technique that most appeals to you

2. Study it

3. Follow directions

4. Breathe a lot

WAYS TO PREVENT FAILURE

Locate a quiet and convenient place to practice

Be consistent

Manage expectations

Breathe a lot

MEDITATION GOALS

1. Stress-free living

2. Pain management

3. Perspective

4. Enlightenment

5. Other

FOR THE WEEK OF: ⬭

LEVEL OF:

RESISTANCE
☐ Kicking / screaming
☐ Mildly hesitant
☐ Mildly intrigued
☐ Curious
☐ Already an old pro

DIFFICULTY
☐ Sheer torture
☐ Herculean
☐ Formidable
☐ Manageable
☐ Child's play

ENJOYMENT
☐ Ecstatic
☐ Revelatory
☐ Harmless
☐ Irritating
☐ Cheerless

BENEFITS	DRAWBACKS
1.	1.
2.	2.
3.	3.

OVERALL IMPRESSION

☐ INSTANT NIRVANA   ☐ SOME (SELF-) IMPROVEMENT   ☐ MEH

FIX-YOURSELF FACT

One of meditation's most unlikely cheerleaders is film director David Lynch, who founded the (aptly titled) David Lynch Foundation to teach at-risk populations of disadvantaged teenagers, veterans, and prisoners how to meditate in order to reduce stress.

VISIT AN ACUPUNCTURIST

☐ NEEDLES ☐ HERBS ☐ MOXIBUSTION

WHAT IS ACUPUNCTURE?

The ancient Chinese medical practice of inserting fine needles into pressure points. Acupuncture treatments also often involve herbal remedies and moxibustion, which stimulates pressure points with heat.

WHY DO IT?

Acupuncture has been linked to relief from chronic conditions such as persistent headaches, lower back pain, and depression.

WHAT TO DO

1. Find a local licensed acupuncturist

2. Make an appointment

3. Attend appointment

4. Get poked

WAYS TO PREVENT FAILURE

Identify particular ailments you want to target

Address needle phobia

Get a referral

Turn off your cell phone

ACUPUNCTURE GOALS

1. Tension relief

2. Ailment alleviation

3. New experience

4. Masochistic indulgence

5. Other

FOR THE WEEK OF:

LEVEL OF:

RESISTANCE
- ☐ Kicking / screaming
- ☐ Mildly hesitant
- ☐ Mildly intrigued
- ☐ Curious
- ☐ Already an old pro

DIFFICULTY
- ☐ Sheer torture
- ☐ Herculean
- ☐ Formidable
- ☐ Manageable
- ☐ Child's play

ENJOYMENT
- ☐ Ecstatic
- ☐ Revelatory
- ☐ Harmless
- ☐ Irritating
- ☐ Cheerless

BENEFITS	DRAWBACKS
1.	1.
2.	2.
3.	3.

OVERALL IMPRESSION

☐ INSTANT NIRVANA ☐ SOME (SELF-) IMPROVEMENT ☐ MEH

FIX-YOURSELF FACT

Acupuncture is getting wild. Veterinary acupuncturists claim the ancient practice can actually be *more* effective on animals than humans. Why? Because cats and dogs aren't stressed out about the cost of treatment.

TAKE CARE OF YOUR ORAL HYGIENE

☐ BRUSH   ☐ FLOSS   ☐ SEE DENTIST

WHAT IS ORAL HYGIENE?

The care and cleaning of your teeth and mouth.

WHY DO IT?

Proper dental care is necessary to avoid painful and unsightly gum disease, tooth loss, and expensive reconstructive surgery. Studies also suggest a connection between oral health and heart disease.

WHAT TO DO

1. Brush at least twice a day
2. Floss daily
3. Schedule dentist appointment
4. Go to appointment

WAYS TO PREVENT FAILURE

Replace your toothbrush every three months

Use flossing picks

Ask for laughing gas at the dentist

Reduce sugar intake

ORAL HYGIENE GOALS

1. Disease-free mouth
2. Denture avoidance
3. Good breath
4. Parental approval
5. Other

FOR THE WEEK OF: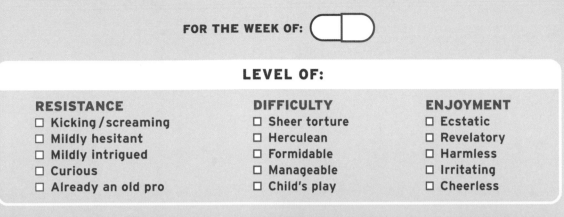

LEVEL OF:

RESISTANCE
- ☐ Kicking / screaming
- ☐ Mildly hesitant
- ☐ Mildly intrigued
- ☐ Curious
- ☐ Already an old pro

DIFFICULTY
- ☐ Sheer torture
- ☐ Herculean
- ☐ Formidable
- ☐ Manageable
- ☐ Child's play

ENJOYMENT
- ☐ Ecstatic
- ☐ Revelatory
- ☐ Harmless
- ☐ Irritating
- ☐ Cheerless

BENEFITS	DRAWBACKS
1.	1.
2.	2.
3.	3.

OVERALL IMPRESSION

☐ INSTANT NIRVANA   ☐ SOME (SELF-) IMPROVEMENT   ☐ MEH

FIX-YOURSELF FACT

Teeth can be as reliable an identifier as fingerprints or DNA. Based on positioning, surface structure, and any restorative work (such as fillings and crowns), it's even possible to distinguish between identical twins.

TALK ABOUT YOUR FEELINGS

☐ TO FRIENDS   ☐ TO FAMILY   ☐ TO THE BARISTA

WHAT IS TALKING ABOUT YOUR FEELINGS?

Verbally communicating how you feel to another person.

WHY DO IT?

Expressing and naming your emotions promotes psychological well-being, increases disease immunity, and strengthens human bonds.

WHAT TO DO

1. Identify an appropriate listener

2. Open your mouth

3. Say how you feel

4. Listen to response

WAYS TO PREVENT FAILURE

Avoid self-censoring

Don't be defensive

Find a good listener

Return the favor

COMMUNICATION GOALS

1. Lighter shoulders

2. Human connection

3. Improved mood

4. Good bitch session

5. Other

FOR THE WEEK OF: ⬭

LEVEL OF:

RESISTANCE
- ☐ Kicking/screaming
- ☐ Mildly hesitant
- ☐ Mildly intrigued
- ☐ Curious
- ☐ Already an old pro

DIFFICULTY
- ☐ Sheer torture
- ☐ Herculean
- ☐ Formidable
- ☐ Manageable
- ☐ Child's play

ENJOYMENT
- ☐ Ecstatic
- ☐ Revelatory
- ☐ Harmless
- ☐ Irritating
- ☐ Cheerless

BENEFITS	DRAWBACKS
1.	1.
2.	2.
3.	3.

OVERALL IMPRESSION

☐ INSTANT NIRVANA   ☐ SOME (SELF-) IMPROVEMENT   ☐ MEH

FIX-YOURSELF FACT

In 1920s Berlin, reclining on a couch in front of company was considered scandalous.
Sigmund Freud used this social taboo to his advantage by setting his patients
on edge and thus encouraging free association during therapy sessions.

DO SOME "FUN" EXERCISE

☐ ZUMBA   ☐ SURFING   ☐ ICE SKATING

WHAT IS "FUN" EXERCISE?

A recreational but physically rigorous activity.

WHY DO IT?

You're more likely to sustain a physically demanding practice if you enjoy it.

WHAT TO DO

1. Pick an activity

2. Obtain any necessary gear and/or enroll in class

3. Perform activity/attend class

4. Have fun

WAYS TO PREVENT FAILURE

Pick a non-embarrassing activity

Have a sense of humor

Bring a friend

Avoid fanny packs

"FUN"-EXERCISE GOALS

1. Improved health

2. Good time

3. Sustainable regime

4. Funny story

5. Other

FOR THE WEEK OF:

LEVEL OF:

RESISTANCE
- ☐ Kicking/screaming
- ☐ Mildly hesitant
- ☐ Mildly intrigued
- ☐ Curious
- ☐ Already an old pro

DIFFICULTY
- ☐ Sheer torture
- ☐ Herculean
- ☐ Formidable
- ☐ Manageable
- ☐ Child's play

ENJOYMENT
- ☐ Ecstatic
- ☐ Revelatory
- ☐ Harmless
- ☐ Irritating
- ☐ Cheerless

BENEFITS	DRAWBACKS
1.	1.
2.	2.
3.	3.

OVERALL IMPRESSION

☐ INSTANT NIRVANA   ☐ SOME (SELF-) IMPROVEMENT   ☐ MEH

FIX-YOURSELF FACT

Swedish physician Gustav Zander established the modern gym's precursor in the late 1800s. Some of the elaborate contraptions invented by Zander actually benefited users' physiques, but many simply massaged or vibrated bodies to little effect.

AVOID MEAT

☐ VEGETARIAN ☐ FLEXITARIAN ☐ VEGAN

WHAT IS AVOIDING MEAT?

Eliminating meat consumption, also known as vegetarianism. Flexitarians eat occasional meat and fish. On the other end of the spectrum, vegans cut out *all* animal-based products, including eggs, honey, and dairy.

WHY DO IT?

Cutting out meat can aid in weight loss and allay health risks associated with heavy meat consumption, including obesity, heart disease, diabetes, and even certain kinds of cancer; vegetarians also spend roughly 20 percent less money than carnivorous shoppers when buying groceries.

WHAT TO DO

1. Stop eating meat

2. Shop at health food stores

3. Cook meals at home

4. Eat plenty of protein

WAYS TO PREVENT FAILURE

Do an Internet search for "slaughterhouse"

Explore seasonings

Eschew steakhouses

Eat vegetables

MEAT-AVOIDING GOALS

1. Weight loss

2. Disease management

3. Cardio benefit

4. Financial benefit

5. Soothed conscience

FOR THE WEEK OF: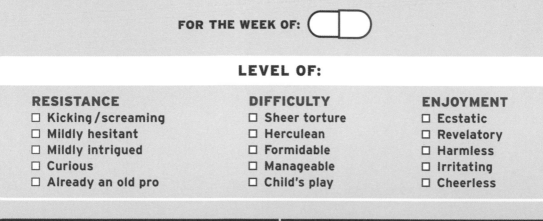

LEVEL OF:

RESISTANCE
- ☐ Kicking/screaming
- ☐ Mildly hesitant
- ☐ Mildly intrigued
- ☐ Curious
- ☐ Already an old pro

DIFFICULTY
- ☐ Sheer torture
- ☐ Herculean
- ☐ Formidable
- ☐ Manageable
- ☐ Child's play

ENJOYMENT
- ☐ Ecstatic
- ☐ Revelatory
- ☐ Harmless
- ☐ Irritating
- ☐ Cheerless

BENEFITS	DRAWBACKS
1.	1.
2.	2.
3.	3.

OVERALL IMPRESSION

☐ INSTANT NIRVANA   ☐ SOME (SELF-) IMPROVEMENT   ☐ MEH

FIX-YOURSELF FACT

When going vegan, beware pitfalls in unexpected places. Gelatin (made with animal by-products) can be found in items as varied as pudding, marshmallows, and capsules. Charred bone is sometimes used to de-colorize cane sugar, and even gum may contain animal-based glycerin.

COMMIT RANDOM ACTS OF KINDNESS

☐ FEED A METER ☐ TIP GENEROUSLY ☐ BRING DONUTS
.

WHAT ARE RANDOM ACTS OF KINDNESS?

Unprovoked altruistic acts conducted with the sole intention of brightening someone else's day.

WHY DO IT?

Altruistic acts are proven to help mitigate stress and improve emotional and physical well-being.

WHAT TO DO

1. Determine feasible random act of kindness

2. Obtain any necessary materials

3. Commit act at random

4. Smile

WAYS TO PREVENT FAILURE

Maintain perspective

Start small

Be on the lookout for opportunities

Don't expect gratitude

KINDNESS GOALS

1. Making someone's day

2. Paying it forward

3. Feeling helpful

4. Filling emotional void

5. Other

FOR THE WEEK OF: ☐☐

LEVEL OF:

RESISTANCE
- ☐ Kicking/screaming
- ☐ Mildly hesitant
- ☐ Mildly intrigued
- ☐ Curious
- ☐ Already an old pro

DIFFICULTY
- ☐ Sheer torture
- ☐ Herculean
- ☐ Formidable
- ☐ Manageable
- ☐ Child's play

ENJOYMENT
- ☐ Ecstatic
- ☐ Revelatory
- ☐ Harmless
- ☐ Irritating
- ☐ Cheerless

BENEFITS	DRAWBACKS
1.	1.
2.	2.
3.	3.

OVERALL IMPRESSION

☐ INSTANT NIRVANA   ☐ SOME (SELF-) IMPROVEMENT   ☐ MEH

FIX-YOURSELF FACT

The ubiquitous bumper-sticker phrase "practice random kindness and senseless acts of beauty" has a complicated story of origin. One theory traces the popular slogan to a 1991 *Glamour* article quoting the writer Anne Herbert, who scrawled it on a placemat while eating in a California diner.

CREATE A SCREAM BOX

☐ CLOSET ☐ BACKSEAT ☐ ACTUAL BOX

WHAT IS A SCREAM BOX?

An enclosed space dedicated to the exclusive purpose of screaming.

WHY DO IT?

Although the effectiveness of screaming as a form of therapy is still controversial, some experts believe that when conducted in a managed environment, screaming can enable you to release anger in a constructive, non-harmful manner.

WHAT TO DO

1. Determine location
2. Assess insulation level
3. Close any doors or windows
4. Scream

WAYS TO PREVENT FAILURE

Drink a throat-coating tea
Manage embarrassment
Identify the source of your frustration
Really let it out

SCREAM BOX GOALS

1. Relief from anger
2. New happy place
3. Outlet for aggression
4. Sultry voice
5. Other

FOR THE WEEK OF: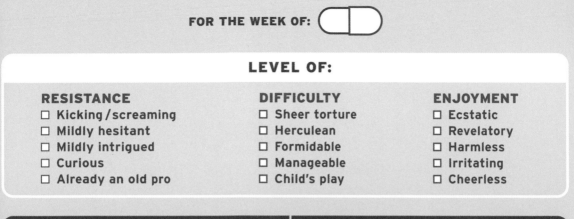

LEVEL OF:

RESISTANCE
- ☐ Kicking / screaming
- ☐ Mildly hesitant
- ☐ Mildly intrigued
- ☐ Curious
- ☐ Already an old pro

DIFFICULTY
- ☐ Sheer torture
- ☐ Herculean
- ☐ Formidable
- ☐ Manageable
- ☐ Child's play

ENJOYMENT
- ☐ Ecstatic
- ☐ Revelatory
- ☐ Harmless
- ☐ Irritating
- ☐ Cheerless

BENEFITS	DRAWBACKS
1.	1.
2.	2.
3.	3.

OVERALL IMPRESSION

☐ INSTANT NIRVANA   ☐ SOME (SELF-) IMPROVEMENT   ☐ MEH

FIX-YOURSELF FACT

Psychologist Arthur Janov wrote *The Primal Scream* in the 1970s, proposing a therapeutic process that involved reliving traumatic events—and lots of screaming. The therapy continues to be practiced today, though the jury is still very much out on its efficacy.

GET A PET

☐ CAT ☐ DOG ☐ FISH

WHAT IS A PET?

An animal kept by people for the purpose of companionship and pleasure.

WHY DO IT?

Studies show that pet owners are more relaxed and have lower blood pressure and fewer incidences of depression than their pet-less counterparts.

WHAT TO DO

1. Visit rescue shelter or website, or responsible breeder/pet store

2. Locate most appealing creature

3. Purchase pet

4. Purchase necessary paraphernalia

5. Care for/enjoy pet

WAYS TO PREVENT FAILURE

Expect time/money commitment

Make sure you're not allergic

Get roommates' OK in advance

Postpone any travel plans

PET OWNERSHIP GOALS

1. Improved mood

2. New buddy

3. Lowered blood pressure

4. Date magnet

5. Other

FOR THE WEEK OF:

LEVEL OF:

RESISTANCE
- ☐ Kicking/screaming
- ☐ Mildly hesitant
- ☐ Mildly intrigued
- ☐ Curious
- ☐ Already an old pro

DIFFICULTY
- ☐ Sheer torture
- ☐ Herculean
- ☐ Formidable
- ☐ Manageable
- ☐ Child's play

ENJOYMENT
- ☐ Ecstatic
- ☐ Revelatory
- ☐ Harmless
- ☐ Irritating
- ☐ Cheerless

BENEFITS

1.

2.

3.

DRAWBACKS

1.

2.

3.

OVERALL IMPRESSION

☐ INSTANT NIRVANA ☐ SOME (SELF-) IMPROVEMENT ☐ MEH

FIX-YOURSELF FACT

Owning a pet can add years to your life. Research has shown that simply petting a dog can decrease blood pressure and stave off depression. Even more impressive, certain dogs have proven capable of "sniffing out" diseases in people, including cancer.

LEARN A MARTIAL ART

☐ KARATE ☐ CAPOIERA ☐ TAI CHI

WHAT IS A MARTIAL ART?

A combative sport involving elements of self-defense, spirituality, and intense discipline.

WHY DO IT?

In addition to the standard benefits of exercise, martial arts may also improve coordination, flexibility, and reflexes.

WHAT TO DO

1. Pick a martial art
2. Locate a nearby dojo/class
3. Obtain appropriate single-color uniform
4. Attend class

WAYS TO PREVENT FAILURE

Research dojo/class ahead of time

Stretch

Watch the original *Karate Kid*

Don't practice in public parks

MARTIAL ARTS GOALS

1. Improved coordination
2. Good workout
3. Self-defense
4. Intimidating chop
5. Other

FOR THE WEEK OF: ⬭

LEVEL OF:

RESISTANCE
☐ Kicking/screaming
☐ Mildly hesitant
☐ Mildly intrigued
☐ Curious
☐ Already an old pro

DIFFICULTY
☐ Sheer torture
☐ Herculean
☐ Formidable
☐ Manageable
☐ Child's play

ENJOYMENT
☐ Ecstatic
☐ Revelatory
☐ Harmless
☐ Irritating
☐ Cheerless

BENEFITS	DRAWBACKS
1.	1.
2.	2.
3.	3.

OVERALL IMPRESSION

☐ INSTANT NIRVANA ☐ SOME (SELF-) IMPROVEMENT ☐ MEH

FIX-YOURSELF FACT

Bruce Lee's interest in martial arts began in the streets of Hong Kong, where he lost a fight to a rival gang member at the age of thirteen. According to legend, it was the last fight he ever lost.

TAP INTO YOUR INNER CHILD

☐ SKIP   ☐ ROLLER SKATE   ☐ GO ON AN ADVENTURE

WHAT IS YOUR INNER CHILD?

An element of the psyche that, according to the theory, is still influenced and determined by experiences and emotions developed during childhood.

WHY DO IT?

Addressing and embracing childlike aspects within your personality can induce pleasurable emotions and behaviors such as wide-eyed enthusiasm and uncontrollable giggling.

WHAT TO DO

1. Identify an activity you enjoyed as a child

2. Obtain parental permission

3. Bring popsicles

4. Proceed with reckless abandon

WAYS TO PREVENT FAILURE

Don't visit playgrounds solo

Avoid swearing

Hydrate with juice boxes

Bring bandages

INNER-CHILD GOALS

1. Inner-child awakening

2. Cardio

3. Laughter

4. Fort-building excuse

5. Other

FOR THE WEEK OF: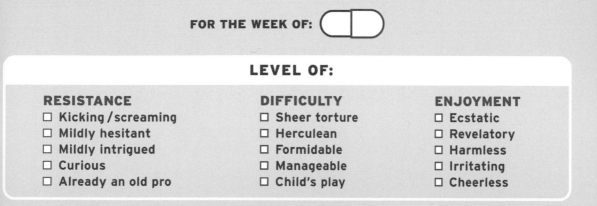

LEVEL OF:

RESISTANCE
- ☐ Kicking/screaming
- ☐ Mildly hesitant
- ☐ Mildly intrigued
- ☐ Curious
- ☐ Already an old pro

DIFFICULTY
- ☐ Sheer torture
- ☐ Herculean
- ☐ Formidable
- ☐ Manageable
- ☐ Child's play

ENJOYMENT
- ☐ Ecstatic
- ☐ Revelatory
- ☐ Harmless
- ☐ Irritating
- ☐ Cheerless

BENEFITS	DRAWBACKS
1.	1.
2.	2.
3.	3.

OVERALL IMPRESSION

☐ INSTANT NIRVANA ☐ SOME (SELF-) IMPROVEMENT ☐ MEH

FIX-YOURSELF FACT

Beloved author Maurice Sendak originally intended to feature horses in his classic picture book *Where the Wild Things Are*. Upon discovering the author couldn't actually draw horses, Sendak's editor suggested using monsters instead (reasoning he could at least draw a "thing").

FACE A FEAR

☐ FLYING   ☐ PUBLIC SPEAKING   ☐ INTIMACY

WHAT IS FEAR-FACING?

Confronting your fears in an attempt to overcome them and stop living in a state of constant terror.

WHY DO IT?

Challenging phobias enables you to transcend feelings of helplessness and affirms personal agency.

WHAT TO DO

1. Identify fear

2. Challenge fear by doing what you fear

3. Take deep breaths

4. Don't freak out

WAYS TO PREVENT FAILURE

Distinguish healthy fears

Take any necessary precautions

Bring a buddy

Swallow pride

FEAR-CONFRONTING GOALS

1. Personal empowerment

2. Cheap thrills

3. Good story

4. Actual transcendence of fear

5. Other

FOR THE WEEK OF:

LEVEL OF:

RESISTANCE	DIFFICULTY	ENJOYMENT
☐ Kicking/screaming	☐ Sheer torture	☐ Ecstatic
☐ Mildly hesitant	☐ Herculean	☐ Revelatory
☐ Mildly intrigued	☐ Formidable	☐ Harmless
☐ Curious	☐ Manageable	☐ Irritating
☐ Already an old pro	☐ Child's play	☐ Cheerless

BENEFITS

1.

2.

3.

DRAWBACKS

1.

2.

3.

OVERALL IMPRESSION

☐ INSTANT NIRVANA   ☐ SOME (SELF-) IMPROVEMENT   ☐ MEH

FIX-YOURSELF FACT

There are far stranger phobias than fearing what goes bump in the night: sufferers of omphalophobia dread bellybuttons, alliumphobes abhor garlic, and peladophobiacs find bald people frightening.

DO YOGA

☐ HATHA ☐ KUNDALINI ☐ BIKRAM

WHAT IS YOGA?

Ancient Indian physical discipline intended to prepare the body for meditation. Known for its contortionist-esque poses and its sweaty, flexible clientele.

WHY DO IT?

Yoga decreases stress, improves physical well-being, and gives you something to be smug about.

WHAT TO DO

1. Buy yoga mat

2. Locate a nearby yoga studio

3. Go to yoga class

4. Follow instructions

WAYS TO PREVENT FAILURE

Go to a beginners' class

Bring a (reusable) bottle of water

Avoid spandex

Breathe

YOGA GOALS

1. Touching of toes

2. Cracking downward dog

3. Hot bod

4. Enlightenment

5. Other

FOR THE WEEK OF: (⬭)

LEVEL OF:

RESISTANCE
- ☐ Kicking/screaming
- ☐ Mildly hesitant
- ☐ Mildly intrigued
- ☐ Curious
- ☐ Already an old pro

DIFFICULTY
- ☐ Sheer torture
- ☐ Herculean
- ☐ Formidable
- ☐ Manageable
- ☐ Child's play

ENJOYMENT
- ☐ Ecstatic
- ☐ Revelatory
- ☐ Harmless
- ☐ Irritating
- ☐ Cheerless

BENEFITS	DRAWBACKS
1.	1.
2.	2.
3.	3.

OVERALL IMPRESSION

☐ INSTANT NIRVANA   ☐ SOME (SELF-) IMPROVEMENT   ☐ MEH

FIX-YOURSELF FACT

Numerous hyper-niche yoga classes have emerged with the rising popularity of yoga in the United States. Tailored to potential yogis' interests, examples include AntiGravity Yoga, nude yoga, circus yoga, and even "doga" (yoga for your dog).

BEHOLD THE POWER OF POSITIVE THINKING!

☐ LEARNED OPTIMISM ☐ CREATIVE VISUALIZATION ☐ FAKE IT 'TIL YOU MAKE IT

WHAT IS POSITIVE THINKING?

Deliberately optimistic thought patterns achieved by disciplined mental focus on what's working in life rather than what's not; can include techniques such as positive self-talk and humor.

WHY DO IT?

Studies have indicated that thinking positively can improve psychological and physical well-being as well as life span.

WHAT TO DO

1. Choose a positive-thinking model

2. Follow instructions

3. Observe your thoughts

4. Think positively

WAYS TO PREVENT FAILURE

Employ affirmations

Don't be discouraged by occasionally pessimistic thoughts

Listen to upbeat music

Stop being so negative

POSITIVE-THINKING GOALS

1. Optimistic outlook

2. Gratitude

3. Less depression

4. Improved health

5. Other

FOR THE WEEK OF:

LEVEL OF:

RESISTANCE
- ☐ Kicking/screaming
- ☐ Mildly hesitant
- ☐ Mildly intrigued
- ☐ Curious
- ☐ Already an old pro

DIFFICULTY
- ☐ Sheer torture
- ☐ Herculean
- ☐ Formidable
- ☐ Manageable
- ☐ Child's play

ENJOYMENT
- ☐ Ecstatic
- ☐ Revelatory
- ☐ Harmless
- ☐ Irritating
- ☐ Cheerless

BENEFITS	DRAWBACKS
1.	1.
2.	2.
3.	3.

OVERALL IMPRESSION

☐ INSTANT NIRVANA ☐ SOME (SELF-) IMPROVEMENT ☐ MEH

FIX-YOURSELF FACT

The bestselling self-help manual *The Secret*, which hypothesizes that positive thinking yields direct results, has sold over 19 million copies and has been translated into more than 40 languages. Clearly *The Secret* works for at least one person—the author, Rhonda Byrne.

WAKE UP EARLY

☐ **BEFORE SUNRISE**   ☐ **SUNRISE**   ☐ **BEFORE NOON**

WHAT IS WAKING UP EARLY?

Opening your eyes, getting out of bed, and (typically) standing up before 7 a.m.

WHY DO IT?

Rising early increases the amount of time in the day to be productive; early morning light is perfect for contemplation as well as very flattering.

WHAT TO DO

1. Set alarm the previous evening for desired wake-up time

2. Wake up

3. Get out of bed

4. Make coffee/tea

WAYS TO PREVENT FAILURE

Go to bed early

Abstain from caffeine the night before

Resist the snooze button

Plan tasty breakfast

WAKE-UP GOALS

1. Viewing of sunrise

2. Reading of paper

3. Greater productivity

4. Sense of righteousness

5. Other

FOR THE WEEK OF:

LEVEL OF:

RESISTANCE
- ☐ Kicking/screaming
- ☐ Mildly hesitant
- ☐ Mildly intrigued
- ☐ Curious
- ☐ Already an old pro

DIFFICULTY
- ☐ Sheer torture
- ☐ Herculean
- ☐ Formidable
- ☐ Manageable
- ☐ Child's play

ENJOYMENT
- ☐ Ecstatic
- ☐ Revelatory
- ☐ Harmless
- ☐ Irritating
- ☐ Cheerless

BENEFITS

1.

2.

3.

DRAWBACKS

1.

2.

3.

OVERALL IMPRESSION

☐ INSTANT NIRVANA   ☐ SOME (SELF-) IMPROVEMENT   ☐ MEH

FIX-YOURSELF FACT

In 2003, researchers at the University of Surrey discovered a gene with both long and short variants that helps regulate the body's internal clock. Individuals with the longer version are more likely to be early birds, while those with the shorter one prefer being night owls.

DRINK (REALLY) FRESH JUICE

☐ VEGETABLE   ☐ FRUIT   ☐ WHEAT GRASS

WHAT IS JUICING?

Drinking freshly made juice in an effort to promote good health.

WHY DO IT?

Juicing is an efficient way to introduce a plethora of vitamins, enzymes, and anti-oxidants to your diet in order to help maintain good health and ward off disease.

WHAT TO DO

1. Purchase a juicer and/or locate convenient juice store
2. Prepare or buy juice
3. Drink juice
4. Slake thirst

WAYS TO PREVENT FAILURE

Avoid esoteric concoctions
Limit intake to mitigate caloric impact
Include palatable ingredients
Drink water, too

JUICING GOALS

1. Improved health
2. Cleansing
3. Pep in step
4. Quenched thirst
5. Other

FOR THE WEEK OF: ⬭

LEVEL OF:

RESISTANCE	DIFFICULTY	ENJOYMENT
☐ Kicking/screaming	☐ Sheer torture	☐ Ecstatic
☐ Mildly hesitant	☐ Herculean	☐ Revelatory
☐ Mildly intrigued	☐ Formidable	☐ Harmless
☐ Curious	☐ Manageable	☐ Irritating
☐ Already an old pro	☐ Child's play	☐ Cheerless

BENEFITS	DRAWBACKS
1.	1.
2.	2.
3.	3.

OVERALL IMPRESSION

☐ INSTANT NIRVANA ☐ SOME (SELF-) IMPROVEMENT ☐ MEH

FIX-YOURSELF FACT

Orange juice is the most popular fruit juice in the United States, but while the super-premium stuff often touts freshness, it doesn't usually win taste tests. Cheaper alternatives tend to fare far better.

TAKE UP GARDENING

☐ ORNAMENTAL   ☐ EDIBLE   ☐ HYDROPONIC

WHAT IS GARDENING?

The act of cultivating vegetation; frequently involves soil, flowers, and utensils such as hoes and watering cans.

WHY DO IT?

Traditional gardening has the same benefits as most forms of exercise, including improved core strength and flexibility as well as reduced stress.

WHAT TO DO

1. Obtain vegetation / seeds

2. Prepare soil

3. Plant things that grow

4. Water vegetation

WAYS TO PREVENT FAILURE

Prune regularly

Mulch

Weed vigilantly

Embrace succulents

GARDENING GOALS

1. Convenient exercise

2. Enhanced environs

3. Organic / cheap produce

4. Available calm

5. Other

FOR THE WEEK OF: ⬭

LEVEL OF:

RESISTANCE
- ☐ Kicking / screaming
- ☐ Mildly hesitant
- ☐ Mildly intrigued
- ☐ Curious
- ☐ Already an old pro

DIFFICULTY
- ☐ Sheer torture
- ☐ Herculean
- ☐ Formidable
- ☐ Manageable
- ☐ Child's play

ENJOYMENT
- ☐ Ecstatic
- ☐ Revelatory
- ☐ Harmless
- ☐ Irritating
- ☐ Cheerless

BENEFITS	DRAWBACKS
1.	1.
2.	2.
3.	3.

OVERALL IMPRESSION

☐ INSTANT NIRVANA   ☐ SOME (SELF-) IMPROVEMENT   ☐ MEH

FIX-YOURSELF FACT

Avoid planting the world's largest flower, the titan arum, better known by its nickname: corpse flower. It grows up to 12 feet tall, can weigh nearly 170 pounds, and smells remarkably like rotting flesh.

DRINK TEA

☐ GREEN   ☐ OOLONG   ☐ KOMBUCHA

WHAT IS TEA?

An ancient beverage of both Chinese and Indian origin made by brewing leaves, herbs, and/or fruits; often associated with various health benefits, relaxation, and British people.

WHY DO IT?

Tea drinking is linked to a variety of health benefits, including but not limited to improved memory and digestion as well as reduced stress.

WHAT TO DO

1. Choose tea

2. Brew tea (if appropriate)

3. Let tea steep

4. Drink tea

WAYS TO PREVENT FAILURE

Locate a good local tea house

Blow on tea that's too hot

Pick out some attractive mugs

Avoid over-steeping

TEA-DRINKING GOALS

1. Coffee/soda replacement

2. Improved health

3. Affordable ritual

4. British affect

5. Other

FOR THE WEEK OF: ☐☐

LEVEL OF:

RESISTANCE
☐ Kicking /screaming
☐ Mildly hesitant
☐ Mildly intrigued
☐ Curious
☐ Already an old pro

DIFFICULTY
☐ Sheer torture
☐ Herculean
☐ Formidable
☐ Manageable
☐ Child's play

ENJOYMENT
☐ Ecstatic
☐ Revelatory
☐ Harmless
☐ Irritating
☐ Cheerless

BENEFITS	DRAWBACKS
1.	1.
2.	2.
3.	3.

OVERALL IMPRESSION

☐ INSTANT NIRVANA ☐ SOME (SELF-) IMPROVEMENT ☐ MEH

FIX-YOURSELF FACT

Whether you choose black, green, oolong, or white tea, you'll still be enjoying the product of a single plant: *camellia sinensis*. The difference in taste is a result of variations in processing or, in the case of white tea, the immaturity of the leaf.

VOLUNTEER

☐ **ANIMAL SHELTER** ☐ **SENIOR CENTER** ☐ **SOUP KITCHEN**

WHAT IS VOLUNTEERING?

Offering time, support, and/or expertise to organizations or individuals.

WHY DO IT?

Volunteering can foster feelings of connection and usefulness,
as well as produce tangible health benefits such as increased
life span and decreased incidence of depression.

WHAT TO DO

1. Identify a cause you relate to

2. Attend orientation

3. Show up on appointed day

4. Help out

WAYS TO PREVENT FAILURE

Think globally, act locally

Avoid bumper-sticker bromides

Do what you can

Give a crap

VOLUNTEERING GOALS

1. Helping others

2. Improved résumé

3. New skill

4. Networking

5. Other

FOR THE WEEK OF:

LEVEL OF:

RESISTANCE	DIFFICULTY	ENJOYMENT
☐ Kicking / screaming	☐ Sheer torture	☐ Ecstatic
☐ Mildly hesitant	☐ Herculean	☐ Revelatory
☐ Mildly intrigued	☐ Formidable	☐ Harmless
☐ Curious	☐ Manageable	☐ Irritating
☐ Already an old pro	☐ Child's play	☐ Cheerless

BENEFITS

1.

2.

3.

DRAWBACKS

1.

2.

3.

OVERALL IMPRESSION

☐ INSTANT NIRVANA   ☐ SOME (SELF-) IMPROVEMENT   ☐ MEH

FIX-YOURSELF FACT

While celebrity volunteers grab headlines, most Americans who help out pursue a quieter altruistic path. According to the Corporation for National and Community Service, fundraising was the most popular charitable act in 2009, followed by food collecting and distribution.

 **FIX-YOURSELF ACTION #21**

BELIEVE IN SOMETHING

☐ THE DIVINE ☐ NATURE ☐ YOURSELF

WHAT IS BELIEF?

A mental state that affirms the truth of a premise; a primary tenet of spiritual faith, it is often employed as a means of comprehending the world outside the self.

WHY DO IT?

Believing in a higher power can take some of the stress out of personal responsibility and lessen angst associated with existential dilemmas.

WHAT TO DO

1. Ponder existence

2. Identify object of reverence

3. Believe in what you revere

4. Pay homage

WAYS TO PREVENT FAILURE

Avoid proselytizing

Acknowledge ambiguities

Keep the faith

Don't worry about celibacy

BELIEF GOALS

1. Improved self-esteem

2. Sense of community

3. Fewer sleepless nights

4. Mortality acceptance

5. Other

FOR THE WEEK OF:

LEVEL OF:

RESISTANCE
- ☐ Kicking / screaming
- ☐ Mildly hesitant
- ☐ Mildly intrigued
- ☐ Curious
- ☐ Already an old pro

DIFFICULTY
- ☐ Sheer torture
- ☐ Herculean
- ☐ Formidable
- ☐ Manageable
- ☐ Child's play

ENJOYMENT
- ☐ Ecstatic
- ☐ Revelatory
- ☐ Harmless
- ☐ Irritating
- ☐ Cheerless

BENEFITS	DRAWBACKS
1.	1.
2.	2.
3.	3.

OVERALL IMPRESSION

☐ INSTANT NIRVANA   ☐ SOME (SELF-) IMPROVEMENT   ☐ MEH

FIX-YOURSELF FACT

According to a study conducted by the Pew Forum on Religion and Public Life,
92 percent of Americans surveyed proclaimed a belief in God or a universal spirit—
even though one in five of the same group self-identified as atheists.

GET A MASSAGE

☐ **SWEDISH**   ☐ **SHIATSU**   ☐ **DEEP TISSUE**

WHAT IS MASSAGE?

The process of kneading and applying pressure to muscle and tissue; frequently associated with relaxation and "release."

WHY DO IT?

Massage is proven to reduce hypertension, decrease symptoms of anxiety and depression, boost immunity, and soothe pain.

WHAT TO DO

1. Choose massage type

2. Locate convenient massage therapist

3. Make appointment

4. Go to appointment

WAYS TO PREVENT FAILURE

Identify the gender of your massage therapist ahead of time

Get a referral

Choose a reputable establishment

Hydrate

MASSAGE GOALS

1. Relaxation

2. Improved outlook

3. Lower blood pressure

4. Pain relief

5. Other

FOR THE WEEK OF: ⬭

LEVEL OF:

RESISTANCE	DIFFICULTY	ENJOYMENT
☐ Kicking/screaming	☐ Sheer torture	☐ Ecstatic
☐ Mildly hesitant	☐ Herculean	☐ Revelatory
☐ Mildly intrigued	☐ Formidable	☐ Harmless
☐ Curious	☐ Manageable	☐ Irritating
☐ Already an old pro	☐ Child's play	☐ Cheerless

BENEFITS	DRAWBACKS
1.	1.
2.	2.
3.	3.

OVERALL IMPRESSION

☐ INSTANT NIRVANA   ☐ SOME (SELF-) IMPROVEMENT   ☐ MEH

FIX-YOURSELF FACT

There over 650 reasons to get a massage—that's the number of muscles in the human body. Together they make up about half a person's weight and outnumber bones three to one.

SELF-MEDICATE

☐ WINE ☐ TV ☐ ROCK AND ROLL

WHAT IS SELF-MEDICATION?

A self-prescribed regimen of behaviors and/or substances
intended to address underlying psychological distress.

WHY DO IT?

Giving yourself permission to mentally check out is necessary every once in a while.

WHAT TO DO

1. Pick a vice

2. Choose appropriate location to indulge

3. Indulge

4. Enjoy

WAYS TO PREVENT FAILURE

Establish boundaries

Consider consequences

Avoid the hard stuff

Drink a lot of water

SELF-MEDICATION GOALS

1. Mental vacation

2. Stress relief

3. Relive the glory days

4. Relate to teenagers

5. Other

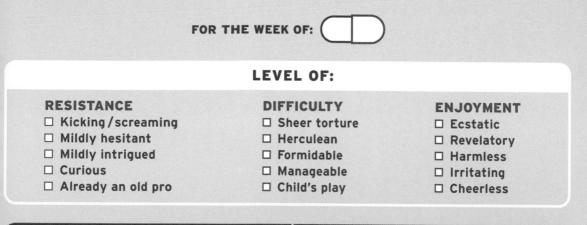

FOR THE WEEK OF:

LEVEL OF:

RESISTANCE
- ☐ Kicking/screaming
- ☐ Mildly hesitant
- ☐ Mildly intrigued
- ☐ Curious
- ☐ Already an old pro

DIFFICULTY
- ☐ Sheer torture
- ☐ Herculean
- ☐ Formidable
- ☐ Manageable
- ☐ Child's play

ENJOYMENT
- ☐ Ecstatic
- ☐ Revelatory
- ☐ Harmless
- ☐ Irritating
- ☐ Cheerless

BENEFITS	DRAWBACKS
1.	1.
2.	2.
3.	3.

OVERALL IMPRESSION

☐ INSTANT NIRVANA ☐ SOME (SELF-) IMPROVEMENT ☐ MEH

FIX-YOURSELF FACT

Although research is ongoing, findings among scientists suggest that red wine can lower a person's chances of heart disease, inhibit high glucose levels, combat obesity, and generally extend one's life. It has also proven to get people drunk.

GO TO THERAPY

☐ COGNITIVE-BEHAVIORAL   ☐ HYPNOSIS   ☐ PSYCHOANALYSIS

WHAT IS THERAPY?

Psychological treatment by a trained professional that targets mental and interpersonal distress and disorders.

WHY DO IT?

Therapy can help you address and modify negative thought and behavior patterns that affect quality of life.

WHAT TO DO

1. Identify nearby licensed therapist

2. Visit therapist

3. Talk

4. Listen

WAYS TO PREVENT FAILURE

Obtain health insurance

Find a therapist you like

Identify target issues

Bring tissue

THERAPY GOALS

1. Crisis management

2. Anxiety alleviation

3. Reduced codependency

4. Saved relationship

5. Other

FOR THE WEEK OF:

LEVEL OF:

RESISTANCE
- ☐ Kicking / screaming
- ☐ Mildly hesitant
- ☐ Mildly intrigued
- ☐ Curious
- ☐ Already an old pro

DIFFICULTY
- ☐ Sheer torture
- ☐ Herculean
- ☐ Formidable
- ☐ Manageable
- ☐ Child's play

ENJOYMENT
- ☐ Ecstatic
- ☐ Revelatory
- ☐ Harmless
- ☐ Irritating
- ☐ Cheerless

BENEFITS	DRAWBACKS
1.	1.
2.	2.
3.	3.

OVERALL IMPRESSION

☐ INSTANT NIRVANA ☐ SOME (SELF-) IMPROVEMENT ☐ MEH

FIX-YOURSELF FACT

Argentina has the most psychologists per capita in the world—145 per 100,000 residents, according to one study. There is even a neighborhood in Buenos Aires that is home to so many shrinks it's informally referred to as "Villa Freud."

RIDE A BIKE

☐ MOUNTAIN ☐ RACER ☐ BEACH CRUISER

WHAT IS BIKE RIDING?

Employing a bicycle as a means of transport.

WHY DO IT?

Riding a bike has all the same health benefits of other types of cardio, but is very easy on the joints; it's also a convenient means of transportation.

WHAT TO DO

1. Obtain bicycle and helmet

2. Don helmet

3. Mount bike

4. Pedal

WAYS TO PREVENT FAILURE

Use designated bike lanes

Wear reflective gear

Pay attention to your surroundings

Avoid hills

BIKE-RIDING GOALS

1. Toned legs

2. Avoidance of traffic jams

3. Movement from point A to point B

4. Enjoyment of outdoors

5. Other

FOR THE WEEK OF: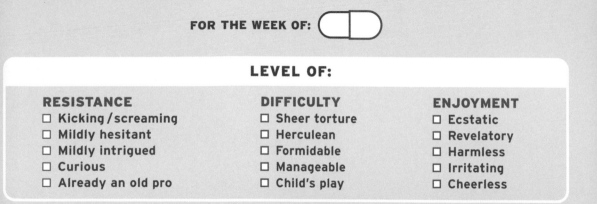

LEVEL OF:

RESISTANCE
- ☐ Kicking/screaming
- ☐ Mildly hesitant
- ☐ Mildly intrigued
- ☐ Curious
- ☐ Already an old pro

DIFFICULTY
- ☐ Sheer torture
- ☐ Herculean
- ☐ Formidable
- ☐ Manageable
- ☐ Child's play

ENJOYMENT
- ☐ Ecstatic
- ☐ Revelatory
- ☐ Harmless
- ☐ Irritating
- ☐ Cheerless

BENEFITS	DRAWBACKS
1.	1.
2.	2.
3.	3.

OVERALL IMPRESSION

☐ INSTANT NIRVANA ☐ SOME (SELF-) IMPROVEMENT ☐ MEH

FIX-YOURSELF FACT

Perhaps the world's most expensive bicycle was ridden by Lance Armstrong during the final leg of the 2009 Tour de France. Created by British artist Damien Hirst, it featured real butterfly wings and fetched half a million dollars at a Sotheby's auction held to benefit various cancer charities.

TAKE A VOW OF SILENCE

☐ WEEK ☐ DAY ☐ HOUR

WHAT IS A VOW OF SILENCE?

A commitment to refrain from talking for a set amount of time, often undertaken in an attempt to have a spiritually significant experience.

WHY DO IT?

Remaining silent can promote contemplation and force practitioners to focus inward; silence also alleviates the pressure to be witty when engaged in conversation.

WHAT TO DO

1. Choose a timeframe for silence

2. Inform others of impending silence

3. Close mouth

4. Don't talk

WAYS TO PREVENT FAILURE

Take time off work

Turn off your phone

Carry a pen and paper with you

Learn some sign language

SILENCE GOALS

1. Peace and quiet

2. Religious experience

3. Rested vocal chords

4. Contemplation

5. Other

FOR THE WEEK OF:

LEVEL OF:

RESISTANCE
- ☐ Kicking/screaming
- ☐ Mildly hesitant
- ☐ Mildly intrigued
- ☐ Curious
- ☐ Already an old pro

DIFFICULTY
- ☐ Sheer torture
- ☐ Herculean
- ☐ Formidable
- ☐ Manageable
- ☐ Child's play

ENJOYMENT
- ☐ Ecstatic
- ☐ Revelatory
- ☐ Harmless
- ☐ Irritating
- ☐ Cheerless

BENEFITS	DRAWBACKS
1.	1.
2.	2.
3.	3.

OVERALL IMPRESSION

☐ INSTANT NIRVANA   ☐ SOME (SELF-) IMPROVEMENT   ☐ MEH

FIX-YOURSELF FACT

Vows of silence aren't just for monks. In 1997, a three-year-old British boy pledged never to speak again if his parents made him undergo a tonsil operation—a vow he kept post-surgery for nearly ten years.

MAKE YOUR BED

☐ **FIRST THING**   ☐ **POST-COFFEE**   ☐ **WHEN YOU GET HOME**

WHAT IS BED-MAKING?

Orderly, smooth arrangement of sheets, pillows, and bedspreads atop a bed.

WHY DO IT?

Making your bed daily promotes alacrity and introduces the discipline of habit into your daily routine, thereby setting a productive tone for the rest of the day.

WHAT TO DO

1. Get out of bed

2. Tuck edges of top sheet and blanket

3. Position pillows

4. Conduct necessary fluffing

WAYS TO PREVENT FAILURE

Obtain desirable sheets and bedspread

Wake up on time

Wash your sheets at least twice a month

Remove detritus

BED-MAKING GOALS

1. A made bed

2. Sense of accomplishment

3. Example setting

4. Cleaner room

5. Other

FOR THE WEEK OF: ⬭

LEVEL OF:

RESISTANCE
- ☐ Kicking/screaming
- ☐ Mildly hesitant
- ☐ Mildly intrigued
- ☐ Curious
- ☐ Already an old pro

DIFFICULTY
- ☐ Sheer torture
- ☐ Herculean
- ☐ Formidable
- ☐ Manageable
- ☐ Child's play

ENJOYMENT
- ☐ Ecstatic
- ☐ Revelatory
- ☐ Harmless
- ☐ Irritating
- ☐ Cheerless

BENEFITS	DRAWBACKS
1.	1.
2.	2.
3.	3.

OVERALL IMPRESSION

☐ INSTANT NIRVANA   ☐ SOME (SELF-) IMPROVEMENT   ☐ MEH

FIX-YOURSELF FACT

You still have to make the bed—even if your dad is president of the United States. First Lady Michelle Obama told reporters that it's a house rule, but also clarified that it "doesn't have to look good—just throw the sheet over it."

FIX-YOURSELF ACTION #28

BREATHE

☐ DIAPHRAGMATIC   ☐ YOGIC   ☐ INTO A PAPER BAG

WHAT IS BREATHING?

A biological process that occurs when air is inhaled, circulated through the lungs, and exhaled.

WHY DO IT?

Certain kinds of concentrated breathing techniques can help with relaxation and focus; it's also necessary for survival.

WHAT TO DO

1. Determine which breathing technique is right for you

2. Inhale

3. Exhale

4. Repeat

WAYS TO PREVENT FAILURE

Don't smoke

Pay attention to your breath

Set aside a certain amount of time

Avoid carbon monoxide

BREATHING GOALS

1. Reduced anxiety

2. Increased attention span

3. Mental reprieve

4. Survival

5. Other

FOR THE WEEK OF: ⬭

LEVEL OF:

RESISTANCE	**DIFFICULTY**	**ENJOYMENT**
☐ Kicking/screaming	☐ Sheer torture	☐ Ecstatic
☐ Mildly hesitant	☐ Herculean	☐ Revelatory
☐ Mildly intrigued	☐ Formidable	☐ Harmless
☐ Curious	☐ Manageable	☐ Irritating
☐ Already an old pro	☐ Child's play	☐ Cheerless

BENEFITS	**DRAWBACKS**
1.	1.
2.	2.
3.	3.

OVERALL IMPRESSION

☐ INSTANT NIRVANA ☐ SOME (SELF-) IMPROVEMENT ☐ MEH

FIX-YOURSELF FACT

Studies have shown that we don't yawn in response to a lack of oxygen, which many assume, and new research has proven inconclusive as well. Scientists have confirmed, however, that we do in fact yawn more when bored.

VISIT A PSYCHIC

☐ PALM READER   ☐ CLAIRVOYANT   ☐ TAROT CARD READER

WHAT ARE PSYCHICS?

People who claim to harness extrasensory perception with which they gather insight, predict future occurrences, communicate with the dead, and perform various other metaphysical feats.

WHY DO IT?

Maybe they know something you don't.

WHAT TO DO

1. Choose psychic
2. Visit psychic
3. Listen to psychic
4. Don't get too carried away

WAYS TO PREVENT FAILURE

Avoid mystics who use neon signage

Pick an affordable medium

Don't trust literal crystal balls

Don't rule out free will

PSYCHIC GOALS

1. Knowledge of the future
2. Insight
3. Communication with dead people
4. Why not?
5. Other

FOR THE WEEK OF: ⬭

LEVEL OF:

RESISTANCE
- ☐ Kicking/screaming
- ☐ Mildly hesitant
- ☐ Mildly intrigued
- ☐ Curious
- ☐ Already an old pro

DIFFICULTY
- ☐ Sheer torture
- ☐ Herculean
- ☐ Formidable
- ☐ Manageable
- ☐ Child's play

ENJOYMENT
- ☐ Ecstatic
- ☐ Revelatory
- ☐ Harmless
- ☐ Irritating
- ☐ Cheerless

BENEFITS	DRAWBACKS
1.	1.
2.	2.
3.	3.

OVERALL IMPRESSION

☐ INSTANT NIRVANA   ☐ SOME (SELF-) IMPROVEMENT   ☐ MEH

FIX-YOURSELF FACT

Sea shanties were sung by nineteenth-century sailors in order to help synchronize complex movements like rope-hauling, sail-setting, and weighing at anchor.

UNPLUG

☐ **CELL PHONE**   ☐ **COMPUTER**   ☐ **TV**

WHAT IS UNPLUGGING?

A conscious effort to reduce dependence on technology by curbing or eliminating the use of digital and electronic devices.

WHY DO IT?

Removing digital distractions from daily life can increase your focus and provide you with more time to communicate face-to-face, thereby fostering a sense of connection and community.

WHAT TO DO

1. Block out time to unplug

2. Turn off applicable electronic devices

3. Don't turn them back on

4. Amuse yourself

WAYS TO PREVENT FAILURE

Warn colleagues, friends, and family beforehand

Turn on auto-reply function

Literally unplug or turn off devices

Embrace paper communication tools

UNPLUGGING GOALS

1. Sanity

2. Decreased sense of responsibility

3. Book reading

4. Carpel-tunnel relief

5. Other

FOR THE WEEK OF: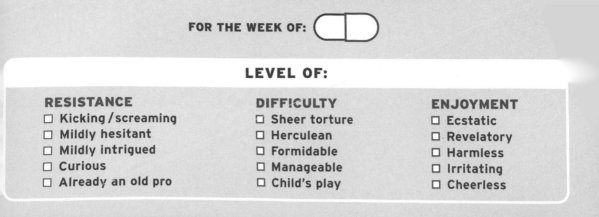

LEVEL OF:

RESISTANCE	DIFFICULTY	ENJOYMENT
☐ Kicking/screaming	☐ Sheer torture	☐ Ecstatic
☐ Mildly hesitant	☐ Herculean	☐ Revelatory
☐ Mildly intrigued	☐ Formidable	☐ Harmless
☐ Curious	☐ Manageable	☐ Irritating
☐ Already an old pro	☐ Child's play	☐ Cheerless

BENEFITS	DRAWBACKS
1.	1.
2.	2.
3.	3.

OVERALL IMPRESSION

☐ INSTANT NIRVANA   ☐ SOME (SELF-) IMPROVEMENT   ☐ MEH

FIX-YOURSELF FACT

While unplugging can be a challenge for adults, it's nearly impossible for today's youth. A recent study by the Kaiser Family Foundation claims that the average teen spends more than seven and a half hours a day plugged in.

CREATE A RELAXATION RITUAL

☐ BUBBLE BATH ☐ EVENING WALK ☐ HAPPY HOUR

WHAT ARE RELAXATION RITUALS?

Symbolic repeated actions and/or activities undertaken to promote a sense of calm, balance, and well-being.

WHY DO IT?

Rituals can promote contemplation and reflection by assigning significance to particular, manageable, and consistent action steps.

WHAT TO DO

1. Choose appealing ritual

2. Buy necessary accessories

3. Designate time to perform ritual

4. Perform ritual

WAYS TO PREVENT FAILURE

Pick something you enjoy

Aim for affordability

Commit to it

Avoid distractions

RELAXATION-RITUAL GOALS

1. Actual relaxation

2. Softer skin

3. Lower blood pressure

4. Excuse to drink wine

5. Other

FOR THE WEEK OF: ⬭

LEVEL OF:

RESISTANCE
☐ Kicking / screaming
☐ Mildly hesitant
☐ Mildly intrigued
☐ Curious
☐ Already an old pro

DIFFICULTY
☐ Sheer torture
☐ Herculean
☐ Formidable
☐ Manageable
☐ Child's play

ENJOYMENT
☐ Ecstatic
☐ Revelatory
☐ Harmless
☐ Irritating
☐ Cheerless

BENEFITS	DRAWBACKS
1.	1.
2.	2.
3.	3.

OVERALL IMPRESSION

☐ INSTANT NIRVANA   ☐ SOME (SELF-) IMPROVEMENT   ☐ MEH

FIX-YOURSELF FACT

According to the American Institute of Stress, the leading cause of stress is the workplace. Google employees may be a happy exception—some of their international offices boast amenities such as quiet rooms, "MetroNap Energy Pods," and free on-site laundry services.

CONSULT A GURU

☐ SHAMANIC ☐ FINANCIAL ☐ CHARISMATIC

WHAT IS A GURU?

A person endowed with wisdom and / or great intelligence who usually dispenses advice of some kind.

WHY DO IT?

Other people can often provide perspective and guidance, ultimately prompting your own insight into how you may better yourself.

WHAT TO DO

1. Find guru to consult

2. Talk to guru

3. Keep an open mind while talking to guru

4. Ponder what guru said

WAYS TO PREVENT FAILURE

Find a likeable guru

Be relatively skeptical

Avoid cults

Seriously, avoid cults

GURU GOALS

1. Wisdom

2. Decent conversation

3. Enlightenment

4. Free rent at commune

5. Other

FOR THE WEEK OF:

LEVEL OF:

RESISTANCE
☐ Kicking / screaming
☐ Mildly hesitant
☐ Mildly intrigued
☐ Curious
☐ Already an old pro

DIFFICULTY
☐ Sheer torture
☐ Herculean
☐ Formidable
☐ Manageable
☐ Child's play

ENJOYMENT
☐ Ecstatic
☐ Revelatory
☐ Harmless
☐ Irritating
☐ Cheerless

BENEFITS

1.
2.
3.

DRAWBACKS

1.
2.
3.

OVERALL IMPRESSION

☐ INSTANT NIRVANA   ☐ SOME (SELF-) IMPROVEMENT   ☐ MEH

FIX-YOURSELF FACT

The word "guru" comes from the Sanskrit word for "venerable." Though its meaning has been loosely interpreted over the years, the traditional Hindu definition is a person who communicates spiritual guidance via oral teachings in an attempt to enlighten students (aka "followers").

MOVE THOSE LEGS

☐ WALK   ☐ JOG   ☐ TAKE THE STAIRS

WHAT IS LEG USE?

Physically engaging the lower limbs.

WHY DO IT?

Even moderate cardiovascular exercise can promote weight loss, increase bone density, improve sleep, reduce anxiety and disease susceptibility, as well as generally enhance self-esteem.

WHAT TO DO

1. Don appropriate garments
2. Choose appealing form of exercise
3. Locate appropriate venue
4. Move legs accordingly

WAYS TO PREVENT FAILURE

Pace yourself

Wear comfortable shoes

Drink water

Avoid the couch

LEG-MOVING GOALS

1. Weight loss
2. Cardiovascular health
3. Improved mood
4. Toned butt
5. Other

FOR THE WEEK OF:

LEVEL OF:

RESISTANCE	DIFFICULTY	ENJOYMENT
☐ Kicking/screaming	☐ Sheer torture	☐ Ecstatic
☐ Mildly hesitant	☐ Herculean	☐ Revelatory
☐ Mildly intrigued	☐ Formidable	☐ Harmless
☐ Curious	☐ Manageable	☐ Irritating
☐ Already an old pro	☐ Child's play	☐ Cheerless

BENEFITS

1.

2.

3.

DRAWBACKS

1.

2.

3.

OVERALL IMPRESSION

☐ INSTANT NIRVANA ☐ SOME (SELF-) IMPROVEMENT ☐ MEH

FIX-YOURSELF FACT

Entertainers including Betty Grable, Fred Astaire, Mary Hart, Angie Everhart, and Michael Flatley have all had their legs insured for at least a million dollars, but soccer player David Beckham may top the list. In 2006, he had his body covered for up to a whopping 100 million British pounds.

GO ORGANIC

☐ COMESTIBLES ☐ HOUSEHOLD/PERSONAL PRODUCTS ☐ FUEL/ENERGY

WHAT IS GOING ORGANIC?

Following ecologically sustainable practices that utilize natural materials and eschew synthetic or artificially derived ingredients and materials.

WHY DO IT?

Organic foods and products contain fewer harmful toxins; consuming organic goods reduces exposure to pesticides, which may decrease susceptibility to certain diseases.

WHAT TO DO

1. Decide on an area to target

2. Visit eco-conscious store

3. Read labels

4. Make purchases

WAYS TO PREVENT FAILURE

Check out the local farmers' market

Identify easily substituted food and goods

Do your research

Don't get preachy about it

ORGANIC GOALS

1. Reduced toxic buildup

2. Support of sustainable businesses

3. Better health

4. Reduced eco-guilt

5. Other

FOR THE WEEK OF: ⬭

LEVEL OF:

RESISTANCE
- ☐ Kicking / screaming
- ☐ Mildly hesitant
- ☐ Mildly intrigued
- ☐ Curious
- ☐ Already an old pro

DIFFICULTY
- ☐ Sheer torture
- ☐ Herculean
- ☐ Formidable
- ☐ Manageable
- ☐ Child's play

ENJOYMENT
- ☐ Ecstatic
- ☐ Revelatory
- ☐ Harmless
- ☐ Irritating
- ☐ Cheerless

BENEFITS	DRAWBACKS
1.	1.
2.	2.
3.	3.

OVERALL IMPRESSION

☐ INSTANT NIRVANA   ☐ SOME (SELF-) IMPROVEMENT   ☐ MEH

FIX-YOURSELF FACT

The Environmental Working Group has identified the "Dirty Dozen": the most important fruits and vegetables to buy organic due to their high pesticide levels when conventionally grown. The list includes favorites such as apples, celery, strawberries, peaches, spinach, potatoes, and lettuce.

ASK FOR HELP

☐ AT WORK   ☐ AT HOME   ☐ AT RANDOM

WHAT IS ASKING FOR HELP?

Engaging another person to assist you in some way.

WHY DO IT?

Seeking support may help to strengthen human bonding, thereby increasing your general sense of well-being; also, you may genuinely need help.

WHAT TO DO

1. Determine needed assistance

2. Seek out trusted individual

3. Open mouth

4. Ask for help

WAYS TO PREVENT FAILURE

Ask pre-frustration

Don't fall into shame spiral

Don't whine

Say thanks

HELP-SEEKING GOALS

1. Lightened load

2. Bonding

3. Balance

4. Relief of "giver" tendencies

5. Other

FOR THE WEEK OF: ⬭

LEVEL OF:

RESISTANCE
- ☐ Kicking/screaming
- ☐ Mildly hesitant
- ☐ Mildly intrigued
- ☐ Curious
- ☐ Already an old pro

DIFFICULTY
- ☐ Sheer torture
- ☐ Herculean
- ☐ Formidable
- ☐ Manageable
- ☐ Child's play

ENJOYMENT
- ☐ Ecstatic
- ☐ Revelatory
- ☐ Harmless
- ☐ Irritating
- ☐ Cheerless

BENEFITS	DRAWBACKS
1.	1.
2.	2.
3.	3.

OVERALL IMPRESSION

☐ INSTANT NIRVANA ☐ SOME (SELF-) IMPROVEMENT ☐ MEH

FIX-YOURSELF FACT

The first so-called advice column dates back to the 1690s. Readers of the *Athenian Mercury* queried the British magazine's "agony" column on matters such as public scandal, etiquette, and temptation. Contemporary advice columnists are still sometimes called "agony aunts" in the UK.

HAVE SEX

☐ GET SOME ☐ GET MORE ☐ DIY

WHAT IS SEX?

The physical reproductive act or associated intimate activities, often performed for purposes of pleasure.

WHY DO IT?

Besides being a biological imperative, sex also relieves stress, boosts immunity, reduces pain, and increases self-esteem.

WHAT TO DO

1. Determine participants

2. Obtain consent

3. Go to private place

4. Merge genitals and/or relevant body parts

WAYS TO PREVENT FAILURE

Engage in foreplay

Use appropriate protection

Avoid excessive whiskey

Don't do it if you don't want to

SEX GOALS

1. Increased quantity

2. Increased quality

3. Experimentation

4. Loss of all shame

5. Other

FOR THE WEEK OF:

LEVEL OF:

RESISTANCE
- ☐ Kicking/screaming
- ☐ Mildly hesitant
- ☐ Mildly intrigued
- ☐ Curious
- ☐ Already an old pro

DIFFICULTY
- ☐ Sheer torture
- ☐ Herculean
- ☐ Formidable
- ☐ Manageable
- ☐ Child's play

ENJOYMENT
- ☐ Ecstatic
- ☐ Revelatory
- ☐ Harmless
- ☐ Irritating
- ☐ Cheerless

BENEFITS	DRAWBACKS
1.	1.
2.	2.
3.	3.

OVERALL IMPRESSION

☐ INSTANT NIRVANA ☐ SOME (SELF-) IMPROVEMENT ☐ MEH

FIX-YOURSELF FACT

According to a 2008 survey conducted by the condom company Durex, two-thirds of Americans believe they're not having enough sex—though not for lack of trying.

SIMPLIFY AND DECLUTTER

□ CLOSET □ SCHEDULE □ FINANCES

WHAT IS SIMPLE LIVING?

A social movement that challenges consumerism by advocating a pared-down lifestyle.

WHY DO IT?

Having fewer choices, possessions, and commitments can reduce
stress and the sense of being overwhelmed.

WHAT TO DO

1. Assess sources of clutter and/or stress

2. Identify actual needs

3. Prune accordingly

4. Gloat

WAYS TO PREVENT FAILURE

Start small

Practice saying no

Keep only what's really important to you

Avoid asceticism

SIMPLIFICATION GOALS

1. Less stress

2. Less stuff

3. Anti-consumerism platform

4. Bird-like freedom

5. Other

FOR THE WEEK OF:

LEVEL OF:

RESISTANCE
- ☐ Kicking/screaming
- ☐ Mildly hesitant
- ☐ Mildly intrigued
- ☐ Curious
- ☐ Already an old pro

DIFFICULTY
- ☐ Sheer torture
- ☐ Herculean
- ☐ Formidable
- ☐ Manageable
- ☐ Child's play

ENJOYMENT
- ☐ Ecstatic
- ☐ Revelatory
- ☐ Harmless
- ☐ Irritating
- ☐ Cheerless

BENEFITS	DRAWBACKS
1.	1.
2.	2.
3.	3.

OVERALL IMPRESSION

☐ INSTANT NIRVANA   ☐ SOME (SELF-) IMPROVEMENT   ☐ MEH

FIX-YOURSELF FACT

Despite espousing the benefits of extreme self-reliance in his seminal simple-living classic, *Walden*, Henry David Thoreau frequently visited his mother during the period of time he writes about—and made sure to bring along his laundry for her to wash.

MAKE A BUCKET LIST

☐ FOR THE YEAR   ☐ FOR THE HELL OF IT   ☐ BEFORE YOU DIE

WHAT IS A BUCKET LIST?

A list that includes (typically) grandiose activities and goals
that you would like to accomplish before you die.

WHY DO IT?

It can inspire action and accomplishment through organization and clear goal setting.

WHAT TO DO

1. Obtain paper and pen

2. Think about stuff you want to do

3. Make list of that stuff

4. Do that stuff

WAYS TO PREVENT FAILURE

Be (somewhat) realistic

Keep your list short

Avoid (mortally) dangerous activities

Do the stuff on your list

BUCKET LIST GOALS

1. Good times

2. Fewer regrets

3. Personal fulfillment

4. Sense of accomplishment

5. Other

FOR THE WEEK OF: ⬭

LEVEL OF:

RESISTANCE
- ☐ Kicking/screaming
- ☐ Mildly hesitant
- ☐ Mildly intrigued
- ☐ Curious
- ☐ Already an old pro

DIFFICULTY
- ☐ Sheer torture
- ☐ Herculean
- ☐ Formidable
- ☐ Manageable
- ☐ Child's play

ENJOYMENT
- ☐ Ecstatic
- ☐ Revelatory
- ☐ Harmless
- ☐ Irritating
- ☐ Cheerless

BENEFITS	DRAWBACKS
1.	1.
2.	2.
3.	3.

OVERALL IMPRESSION

☐ INSTANT NIRVANA   ☐ SOME (SELF-) IMPROVEMENT   ☐ MEH

FIX-YOURSELF FACT

A Florida woman with nonterminal leukemia cited her bucket list as the motivation behind robbing a bank in 2010. She explained to reporters, "I think everyone should have a list of things they want to do before they expire." She also admitted the robbery was the *only* item on her list.

DEPRIVE YOUR SENSES

☐ CHAMBER REST   ☐ DRY FLOTATION REST   ☐ BLINDFOLD/EARMUFFS

WHAT IS SENSORY DEPRIVATION?

Deliberate isolation and removal of external stimuli; often conducted in a chamber built specifically for stated purpose.

WHY DO IT?

Certain sensory deprivation techniques (such as flotation tank therapy) have been proven to reduce stress and chronic pain by mimicking zero-gravity conditions.

WHAT TO DO

1. Pick most appealing technique
2. Schedule appointment or set aside time
3. Deprive senses
4. Relax

WAYS TO PREVENT FAILURE

Pick a safety word

Breathe deeply

Address claustrophobia beforehand

Turn off your cell phone

SENSORY DEPRIVATION GOALS

1. Tranquility
2. Claustrophobia mitigation
3. Pain reduction
4. New experience
5. Other

FOR THE WEEK OF: ⬭

LEVEL OF:

RESISTANCE
☐ Kicking / screaming
☐ Mildly hesitant
☐ Mildly intrigued
☐ Curious
☐ Already an old pro

DIFFICULTY
☐ Sheer torture
☐ Herculean
☐ Formidable
☐ Manageable
☐ Child's play

ENJOYMENT
☐ Ecstatic
☐ Revelatory
☐ Harmless
☐ Irritating
☐ Cheerless

BENEFITS

1.

2.

3.

DRAWBACKS

1.

2.

3.

OVERALL IMPRESSION

☐ INSTANT NIRVANA ☐ SOME (SELF-) IMPROVEMENT ☐ MEH

FIX-YOURSELF FACT

Used to describe the savory "fifth taste" after salty, sweet, sour, and bitter, the term *umami*, Japanese for "yummy," has become a foodie buzzword. Umami is created by the natural breakdown of organic matter; parmesan cheese, soy sauce, and cooked meat are umami.

GO FORTH AND TRAVEL

☐ ROAD TRIP ☐ FARAWAY ADVENTURE ☐ WEEKEND JAUNT

WHAT IS TRAVEL?

A journey to a place other than the location where you live.

WHY DO IT?

Vacations cut the risk of heart attack, reduce stress, and promote a more positive outlook on life; they also provide enjoyable new memories.

WHAT TO DO

1. Pick destination

2. Arrange transportation

3. Pack

4. Depart

WAYS TO PREVENT FAILURE

Pack light

Carry identification

Book accommodations ahead of time

Be flexible

TRAVEL GOALS

1. New experiences

2. Relaxation

3. Renewed optimism

4. Photo ops

5. Other

FOR THE WEEK OF:

LEVEL OF:

RESISTANCE
- ☐ Kicking/screaming
- ☐ Mildly hesitant
- ☐ Mildly intrigued
- ☐ Curious
- ☐ Already an old pro

DIFFICULTY
- ☐ Sheer torture
- ☐ Herculean
- ☐ Formidable
- ☐ Manageable
- ☐ Child's play

ENJOYMENT
- ☐ Ecstatic
- ☐ Revelatory
- ☐ Harmless
- ☐ Irritating
- ☐ Cheerless

BENEFITS	DRAWBACKS
1.	1.
2.	2.
3.	3.

OVERALL IMPRESSION

☐ INSTANT NIRVANA ☐ SOME (SELF-) IMPROVEMENT ☐ MEH

FIX-YOURSELF FACT

France receives over 70 million international tourists annually, making it the world's most visited country. Not surprisingly, the famously romantic city of Paris is the republic's most popular destination.

FIX-YOURSELF ACTION #42

REMEMBER TO SMILE

☐ EVERY THIRTY MINUTES   ☐ EVERY HOUR   ☐ WHEN YOU FEEL LIKE IT

WHAT IS A SMILE?

A facial expression formed by upturned corners of the mouth that signifies pleasure.

WHY DO IT?

Research has verified that smiling increases feel-good chemicals such as serotonin and dopamine in the brain, thereby reducing stress and promoting feelings of relaxation.

WHAT TO DO

1. Contract facial muscles

2. Flex jaw

3. Crinkle eyes

4. Show teeth

WAYS TO PREVENT FAILURE

Think about things that make you happy

Obtain a whitening toothpaste

Spend time with amusing friends

Watch *Ghostbusters*

SMILING GOALS

1. Happiness

2. Relaxation

3. Attracting others

4. Prevention of frown lines

5. Other

FOR THE WEEK OF: ⬭

LEVEL OF:

RESISTANCE
☐ Kicking/screaming
☐ Mildly hesitant
☐ Mildly intrigued
☐ Curious
☐ Already an old pro

DIFFICULTY
☐ Sheer torture
☐ Herculean
☐ Formidable
☐ Manageable
☐ Child's play

ENJOYMENT
☐ Ecstatic
☐ Revelatory
☐ Harmless
☐ Irritating
☐ Cheerless

BENEFITS	DRAWBACKS
1.	1.
2.	2.
3.	3.

OVERALL IMPRESSION

☐ INSTANT NIRVANA   ☐ SOME (SELF-) IMPROVEMENT   ☐ MEH

FIX-YOURSELF FACT

Faking a genuine smile isn't just hard—it's scientifically impossible. An authentic smile is the product of a reflex generated by the limbic system, the brain's emotional center.

RESTRICT YOUR DIET

☐ GLUTEN ☐ SUGAR ☐ BOOZE

WHAT IS DIET RESTRICTION?

Cutting a component from your daily food and beverage consumption for health, religious, medical, social, or vanity-related reasons.

WHY DO IT?

Even removing one food or beverage item from your diet can have a large impact on your physical and/or mental health.

WHAT TO DO

1. Identify item or food group to abstain from

2. Remove item from kitchen

3. Exercise self-control

4. Avoid cookie aisle

WAYS TO PREVENT FAILURE

Choose feasible item(s) to cut

Read labels

Plan ahead

Determine substitutes

DIET-RESTRICTION GOALS

1. Weight loss

2. Improved complexion

3. Soothed stomach

4. Reduced appetite

5. Other

FOR THE WEEK OF: ⬭

LEVEL OF:

RESISTANCE
- ☐ Kicking / screaming
- ☐ Mildly hesitant
- ☐ Mildly intrigued
- ☐ Curious
- ☐ Already an old pro

DIFFICULTY
- ☐ Sheer torture
- ☐ Herculean
- ☐ Formidable
- ☐ Manageable
- ☐ Child's play

ENJOYMENT
- ☐ Ecstatic
- ☐ Revelatory
- ☐ Harmless
- ☐ Irritating
- ☐ Cheerless

BENEFITS	DRAWBACKS
1.	1.
2.	2.
3.	3.

OVERALL IMPRESSION

☐ INSTANT NIRVANA   ☐ SOME (SELF-) IMPROVEMENT   ☐ MEH

FIX-YOURSELF FACT

In a 2010 Scripps Florida study, rats given a steady diet of junk food including Ding Dongs, frosting, and bacon maintained their unhealthy diet even when electrically shocked post-binge. Afterwards, the same rats voluntarily starved themselves rather than eat healthier food options.

FIX-
YOURSELF
ACTION #44

GET A MAKEOVER

☐ CLOTHING   ☐ HAIR   ☐ BODY HAIR

WHAT IS A MAKEOVER?

A physical transformation that changes a person's appearance.

WHY DO IT?

Makeovers can improve confidence and decrease feelings of insecurity.

WHAT TO DO

1. Identify area to change
2. Make appointment with professional
3. Attend appointment
4. Change area identified

WAYS TO PREVENT FAILURE

Make major changes one at a time

Get a referral

Bring a friend

Don't go overboard

MAKEOVER GOALS

1. Healthy hair
2. Glowing skin
3. Improved wardrobe
4. Self-esteem boost
5. Other

FOR THE WEEK OF: ⬭

LEVEL OF:

RESISTANCE	DIFFICULTY	ENJOYMENT
☐ Kicking/screaming	☐ Sheer torture	☐ Ecstatic
☐ Mildly hesitant	☐ Herculean	☐ Revelatory
☐ Mildly intrigued	☐ Formidable	☐ Harmless
☐ Curious	☐ Manageable	☐ Irritating
☐ Already an old pro	☐ Child's play	☐ Cheerless

BENEFITS	DRAWBACKS
1.	1.
2.	2.
3.	3.

OVERALL IMPRESSION

☐ INSTANT NIRVANA ☐ SOME (SELF-) IMPROVEMENT ☐ MEH

FIX-YOURSELF FACT

The prize for the world's most expensive haircut goes to the Sultan Hassanal Bolkiah Mu'izzaddin Waddaulah of Brunei. He flew London barber Ken Modestou 7,000 miles in a private suite aboard a Singapore Airlines flight. All told, the Sultan's deluxe 'do cost approximately $24,000.

WRITE IN A JOURNAL

☐ TRADITIONAL   ☐ DREAM   ☐ GRATITUDE

WHAT IS JOURNALING?

Writing thoughts, impressions, and feelings down in an attempt to process emotions more effectively.

WHY DO IT?

Studies show that consistent journaling improves mental and physical well-being. Also, journals don't get sick of listening.

WHAT TO DO

1. Purchase journal

2. Obtain pen

3. Get comfortable

4. Write for at least fifteen minutes

WAYS TO PREVENT FAILURE

Don't self-censor

Find a safe place to keep your journal

Write every day

Doodle if you must

JOURNALING GOALS

1. Reflection

2. Emotional breakthrough

3. Creative outlet

4. Improved penmanship

5. Other

LEVEL OF:

RESISTANCE
- ☐ Kicking / screaming
- ☐ Mildly hesitant
- ☐ Mildly intrigued
- ☐ Curious
- ☐ Already an old pro

DIFFICULTY
- ☐ Sheer torture
- ☐ Herculean
- ☐ Formidable
- ☐ Manageable
- ☐ Child's play

ENJOYMENT
- ☐ Ecstatic
- ☐ Revelatory
- ☐ Harmless
- ☐ Irritating
- ☐ Cheerless

BENEFITS	DRAWBACKS
1.	1.
2.	2.
3.	3.

OVERALL IMPRESSION

☐ INSTANT NIRVANA   ☐ SOME (SELF-) IMPROVEMENT   ☐ MEH

FIX-YOURSELF FACT

You don't have to be the next James Joyce to reap the mental benefits of journaling; experts agree that as little as five minutes of writing down your thoughts and feelings, quasi-daily, will produce a positive effect.

FIX-YOURSELF ACTION #46

INDULGE IN A LITTLE SCHADENFREUDE

☐ POINT AND LAUGH ☐ WATCH REALITY TV ☐ GOSSIP

WHAT IS SCHADENFREUDE?

A German word for the pleasurable emotions some people feel in response to other people's misfortune or embarrassment.

WHY DO IT?

Other people's difficulties can cause you to reflect positively on your relatively agreeable circumstances.

WHAT TO DO

1. Identify object of schadenfreude
2. Observe the person's failure or misfortune
3. Feel pleasure
4. Try not to feel too bad about it

WAYS TO PREVENT FAILURE

Never cause the misfortune

Don't make it a habit

Target strangers

Keep it light

SCHADENFREUDE GOALS

1. Laughter
2. Self-esteem boost
3. Bonding with fellow observers
4. Loosening of moral standards
5. Other

FOR THE WEEK OF:

LEVEL OF:

RESISTANCE
- ☐ Kicking / screaming
- ☐ Mildly hesitant
- ☐ Mildly intrigued
- ☐ Curious
- ☐ Already an old pro

DIFFICULTY
- ☐ Sheer torture
- ☐ Herculean
- ☐ Formidable
- ☐ Manageable
- ☐ Child's play

ENJOYMENT
- ☐ Ecstatic
- ☐ Revelatory
- ☐ Harmless
- ☐ Irritating
- ☐ Cheerless

BENEFITS	DRAWBACKS
1.	1.
2.	2.
3.	3.

OVERALL IMPRESSION

☐ INSTANT NIRVANA   ☐ SOME (SELF-) IMPROVEMENT   ☐ MEH

FIX-YOURSELF FACT

Schadenfreude combines the German terms for "damage" (*schaden*) and "joy" (*freude*). It's used to describe those occasions when one takes pleasure in another's (often deserved) suffering. The inverted variation "freudenschade" indicates feeling sadness in response to another's happiness.

TAKE UP A HOBBY

☐ POTTERY ☐ MACRAMÉ ☐ GOLF

WHAT IS A HOBBY?

A leisure activity performed for pleasure and relaxation.

WHY DO IT?

Hobbies provide an engaging and rewarding activity to enjoy during leisure time; pursuing creative outlets and outside interests independently from the workplace can lead to a sense of pride and accomplishment.

WHAT TO DO

1. Pick hobby
2. Obtain necessary supplies
3. Read applicable instructions
4. Conduct hobby

WAYS TO PREVENT FAILURE

Set aside an hour every day

Begin with small, manageable projects

Avoid bedazzlers

Apply glitter judiciously

HOBBY GOALS

1. Sense of achievement
2. Fun
3. Handmade accessories
4. Etsy store
5. Other

FOR THE WEEK OF:

LEVEL OF:

RESISTANCE
- ☐ Kicking/screaming
- ☐ Mildly hesitant
- ☐ Mildly intrigued
- ☐ Curious
- ☐ Already an old pro

DIFFICULTY
- ☐ Sheer torture
- ☐ Herculean
- ☐ Formidable
- ☐ Manageable
- ☐ Child's play

ENJOYMENT
- ☐ Ecstatic
- ☐ Revelatory
- ☐ Harmless
- ☐ Irritating
- ☐ Cheerless

BENEFITS	DRAWBACKS
1.	1.
2.	2.
3.	3.

OVERALL IMPRESSION

☐ INSTANT NIRVANA ☐ SOME (SELF-) IMPROVEMENT ☐ MEH

FIX-YOURSELF FACT

Popular hobbies during the Victorian era were often prone to a decidedly macabre bent. To commemorate the loss of a loved one, grieving women sometimes wove the hair of the dearly departed into crafty homemade accessories.

GO TO A 12-STEP MEETING

☐ ALCOHOLICS ANONYMOUS ☐ AL-ANON ☐ OVEREATERS ANONYMOUS

WHAT IS 12-STEP?

A set of guiding principles that aid in recovery from a variety of addictive behaviors. Known for its group meetings, reliance upon a higher power, and church basements.

WHY DO IT?

Twelve-step meetings can be a cathartic and greatly helpful experience for those who suffer from addiction or are affected by other people's addiction.

WHAT TO DO

1. Identify addiction/problematic behavior

2. Locate relevant 12-step meeting

3. Attend 12-step meeting

4. Follow instructions

WAYS TO PREVENT FAILURE

Arrive on time

Have an open mind

Enjoy the coffee and cookies—they're free

Smile

RECOVERY GOALS

1. Cutting down

2. Getting a sponsor

3. Working the steps

4. Making sober friends

5. Other

FOR THE WEEK OF: ◯▢

LEVEL OF:

RESISTANCE
- ☐ Kicking / screaming
- ☐ Mildly hesitant
- ☐ Mildly intrigued
- ☐ Curious
- ☐ Already an old pro

DIFFICULTY
- ☐ Sheer torture
- ☐ Herculean
- ☐ Formidable
- ☐ Manageable
- ☐ Child's play

ENJOYMENT
- ☐ Ecstatic
- ☐ Revelatory
- ☐ Harmless
- ☐ Irritating
- ☐ Cheerless

BENEFITS	DRAWBACKS
1.	1.
2.	2.
3.	3.

OVERALL IMPRESSION

☐ INSTANT NIRVANA   ☐ SOME (SELF-) IMPROVEMENT   ☐ MEH

FIX-YOURSELF FACT

Two former alcoholics founded the first 12-step program, Alcoholics Anonymous, in 1935. Membership rates are hard to track due to the anonymous nature of the organization, but AA is currently estimated to have over two million members and a presence in over 150 countries.

PRACTICE FENG SHUI

☐ BEDROOM ☐ BATHROOM ☐ OFFICE

WHAT IS FENG SHUI?

An ancient Chinese practice of organizing objects, spaces, and architectural structures according to certain spiritual principles.

WHY DO IT?

Supporters claim that feng shui produces good fortune in arenas as diverse as finances and fertility; additionally, it offers a ready justification for redecorating.

WHAT TO DO

1. Research feng shui

2. Move some stuff around room accordingly

3. Wait

4. Experience good luck

WAYS TO PREVENT FAILURE

Work with what you have

Maximize natural light

Don't stress out about it

Manage expectations

FENG SHUI GOALS

1. Interior decoration

2. Balance

3. Aesthetic mastery

4. All-encompassing success

5. Other

FOR THE WEEK OF: ⬭

LEVEL OF:

RESISTANCE
- ☐ Kicking/screaming
- ☐ Mildly hesitant
- ☐ Mildly intrigued
- ☐ Curious
- ☐ Already an old pro

DIFFICULTY
- ☐ Sheer torture
- ☐ Herculean
- ☐ Formidable
- ☐ Manageable
- ☐ Child's play

ENJOYMENT
- ☐ Ecstatic
- ☐ Revelatory
- ☐ Harmless
- ☐ Irritating
- ☐ Cheerless

BENEFITS	DRAWBACKS
1.	1.
2.	2.
3.	3.

OVERALL IMPRESSION

☐ INSTANT NIRVANA ☐ SOME (SELF-) IMPROVEMENT ☐ MEH

FIX-YOURSELF FACT

Feng shui still holds impressive sway in modern China. In 2007, one of the world's wealthiest women, Hong Kong billionaire Nina Wang, passed away and left her entire fortune to her feng shui adviser.

TREAT YOURSELF TO A FAVORITE FOOD

☐ ADD CHEESE ☐ HAVE SECONDS ☐ ORDER DESSERT

WHAT IS TREATING YOURSELF?

Indulging in gastronomical pleasures—without guilt.

WHY DO IT?

Allowing yourself to enjoy food just for the joy of it promotes a healthy attitude toward consumption in general and counteracts feelings of deprivation (which can lead to nutritional sabotage).

WHAT TO DO

1. Pick favorite culinary indulgence

2. Stay present

3. Savor every bite

4. Sigh with pleasure

WAYS TO PREVENT FAILURE

Don't treat yourself every day

Maintain nutritional balance

Check any negative self-talk

Stop when you're full

INDULGENCE GOALS

1. Pleasure

2. Dopamine boost

3. Improved attitude toward food

4. Satiation

5. Other

LEVEL OF:

RESISTANCE
- ☐ Kicking / screaming
- ☐ Mildly hesitant
- ☐ Mildly intrigued
- ☐ Curious
- ☐ Already an old pro

DIFFICULTY
- ☐ Sheer torture
- ☐ Herculean
- ☐ Formidable
- ☐ Manageable
- ☐ Child's play

ENJOYMENT
- ☐ Ecstatic
- ☐ Revelatory
- ☐ Harmless
- ☐ Irritating
- ☐ Cheerless

BENEFITS	DRAWBACKS
1.	1.
2.	2.
3.	3.

OVERALL IMPRESSION

☐ INSTANT NIRVANA   ☐ SOME (SELF-) IMPROVEMENT   ☐ MEH

FIX-YOURSELF FACT

Sometimes the tastiest choice actually *is* the best choice—at least calorically speaking. For example, one cup of granola is liable to have the same number of calories as ten slices of bacon. Similarly, the calorie count of one breakfast bagel is on par with that of two glazed donuts.

GO OUTDOORS

☐ TAKE HIKE ☐ GO TO PARK ☐ SWIM AT BEACH

WHAT IS THE OUTDOORS?

Natural settings that are not enclosed by structures.

WHY DO IT?

Even ten minutes spent outdoors can improve mood and generally contribute to a more positive outlook on life.

WHAT TO DO

1. Identify attractive natural location

2. Arrange transportation

3. Obtain supplies

4. Go outside

WAYS TO PREVENT FAILURE

Don weather-appropriate garb

Bring snacks

Remember the sunscreen

Take along the GPS

OUTDOOR GOALS

1. Relaxation

2. Perspective

3. Fresh air

4. Rose smelling

5. Other

FOR THE WEEK OF:

LEVEL OF:

RESISTANCE
- ☐ Kicking / screaming
- ☐ Mildly hesitant
- ☐ Mildly intrigued
- ☐ Curious
- ☐ Already an old pro

DIFFICULTY
- ☐ Sheer torture
- ☐ Herculean
- ☐ Formidable
- ☐ Manageable
- ☐ Child's play

ENJOYMENT
- ☐ Ecstatic
- ☐ Revelatory
- ☐ Harmless
- ☐ Irritating
- ☐ Cheerless

BENEFITS	DRAWBACKS
1.	1.
2.	2.
3.	3.

OVERALL IMPRESSION

☐ INSTANT NIRVANA   ☐ SOME (SELF-) IMPROVEMENT   ☐ MEH

FIX-YOURSELF FACT

Established in 1968, the National Trails System features nearly 54,000 miles stretching across the fifty states. Trekking the entire distance is equivalent to walking from Los Angeles to New York City over twenty times.

FIX-YOURSELF ACTION #52

PRACTICE ACCEPTANCE

☐ PHYSICAL FLAWS ☐ LIMITATIONS ☐ ENTIRE SELF

WHAT IS ACCEPTANCE?

A psychological state characterized by the absence of protest and any attempt at denial when confronted by a difficult or distressing situation or circumstance.

WHY DO IT?

Sometimes it's all you *can* do.

WHAT TO DO

1. Recognize reality
2. Admit reality
3. Accept reality as it is
4. Keep accepting it

WAYS TO PREVENT FAILURE

Set attainable goals
Understand your limitations
Practice letting go
Try baby steps

ACCEPTANCE GOALS

1. Lessened anxiety
2. Relaxed demeanor
3. Zen-like grace
4. Curbing of control-freak behavior
5. Other

FOR THE WEEK OF: ⬭

LEVEL OF:

RESISTANCE
- ☐ Kicking / screaming
- ☐ Mildly hesitant
- ☐ Mildly intrigued
- ☐ Curious
- ☐ Already an old pro

DIFFICULTY
- ☐ Sheer torture
- ☐ Herculean
- ☐ Formidable
- ☐ Manageable
- ☐ Child's play

ENJOYMENT
- ☐ Ecstatic
- ☐ Revelatory
- ☐ Harmless
- ☐ Irritating
- ☐ Cheerless

BENEFITS	DRAWBACKS
1.	1.
2.	2.
3.	3.

OVERALL IMPRESSION

☐ INSTANT NIRVANA ☐ SOME (SELF-) IMPROVEMENT ☐ MEH

FIX-YOURSELF FACT

Carl Rogers was an influential contributor to humanistic psychology who espoused "unconditional positive regard." Complete acceptance of others is the basis of this affirmative concept that encourages you to accept even yourself—just the way you are.

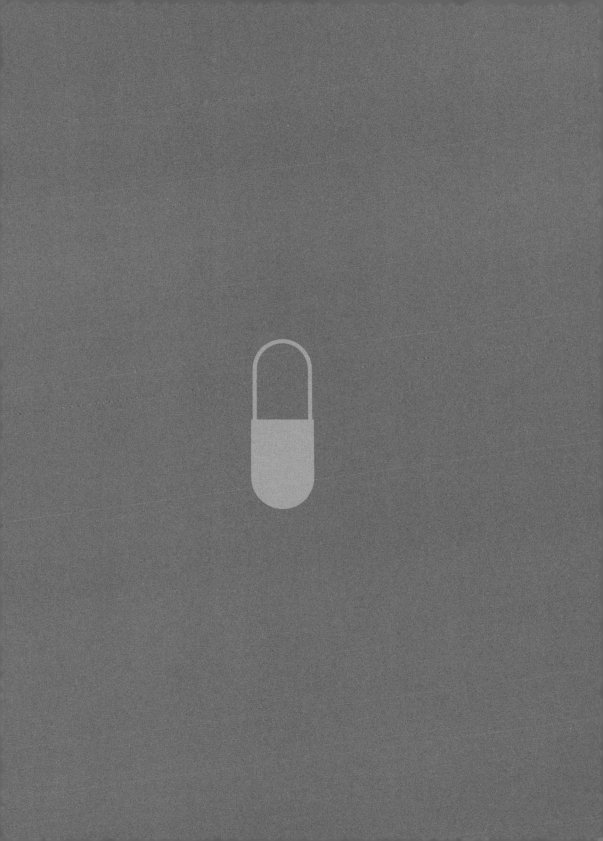